Learning

Our Letters

Learning Our Letters

By Rosene L. Burkholder
Artist: Martha Shertzler Kuhns

Little
JEWEL
Books

Rod and Staff Publishers, Inc.
P. O. Box 3, Hwy. 172
Crockett, Kentucky 41413
Telephone: (606) 522-4348

Copyright 1994

Rod and Staff Publishers, Inc.

Crockett, Kentucky 41413

Printed in U.S.A.

ISBN 978-07399-0050-5

Catalog no. 2580

7   8   9   10   11   —   27   26   25   24   23   22   21   20   19   18

A
B
C
D
E
F
G
H
I
J
K
L
M

N
O
P
Q
R
S
T
U
V
W
X
Y
Z

Aa

A is for a little **ark**;
'Twas baby Moses' boat.
His mother gently tucked him in.
And Miriam watched it float.

B b

B is for a friendly **boy**
　Who gladly shared his food;
Then Jesus blessed the bread and fish,
　And fed the multitude.

Cc

C is for the **camel**. How
It dreads to think of work;
But when it has a job to do,
The camel doesn't shirk.

D is for the **donkey** brave
That Balaam rode one day.
Then all at once an angel came
And blocked the donkey's way.

E e

E is for the **elephant**;
    Just see his ears and toes!
God also gave this animal
    A very useful nose.

F f

F is for the many **fish**
That swim in brook and bay.
A big one swallowed Jonah when
From God he ran away.

G is for a flock of **geese**;
We like to see them go.
They travel south to sunny lands,
Away from cold and snow.

H is for the puppy **house**
We're helping Father build.
We run to get a board or two
And keep his nail bag filled

Ii

I is for the **igloo**, built
    With icy blocks of snow.
The Eskimos are safe inside
    When winter storms will blow.

J j

J is for dear **Jesus**, who
   Was born long ago.
When angels brought the joyful news,
   The shepherds said, Let's go!"

Kk

K is for the **kangaroo**
   That hops on legs so strong.
And everywhere she wants to go,
   Her baby rides along.

L is for the **lizard** I
  Had thought I caught today.
But all at once the tail came off,
  And lizard ran away!

M m

M is for the widow's **mites**–
The only coins she had.
But gratefully she offered them,
And Jesus' heart was glad.

N n

N is for the crunchy **nuts**
The squirrel likes to hide
So he will have some food to eat
When it is cold outside.

O is for the great horned **owl**,
    With feathers brown and white;
It often sleeps while children play,
    And hunts for food at night.

P p

P is for the **penguins**. These
Are birds that cannot fly.
They swim in icy water, but
Their feathers keep them dry.

Q is for a lovely **queen**
 Whose husband was a king;
When Esther saved her people dear,
 She made their sad hearts sing.

R r

R is for the **rabbits** bold;
   They hop on nimble feet.
They go to Mother's lettuce patch
   To get a leafy treat.

S s

S is for the cheery **sun**.
　God hung it out in space
To make the pretty flowers grow,
　And gently warm my face.

T t

T is for the westbound **train**
   That's roaring down the track.
I like to hear the whistle blow;
   I hope it soon comes back.

U u

U is for the **umbrella**. When
  It rains on hill and tree,
I open my umbrella so
  It doesn't rain on me!

V v

V is for the lovely **vines**
That climb above the gate.
The morning glories bloom at dawn,
And never stay up late.

Ww

W is for **watermelon**,
Juicy, red, and sweet.
When summer days are very warm,
I like a piece to eat.

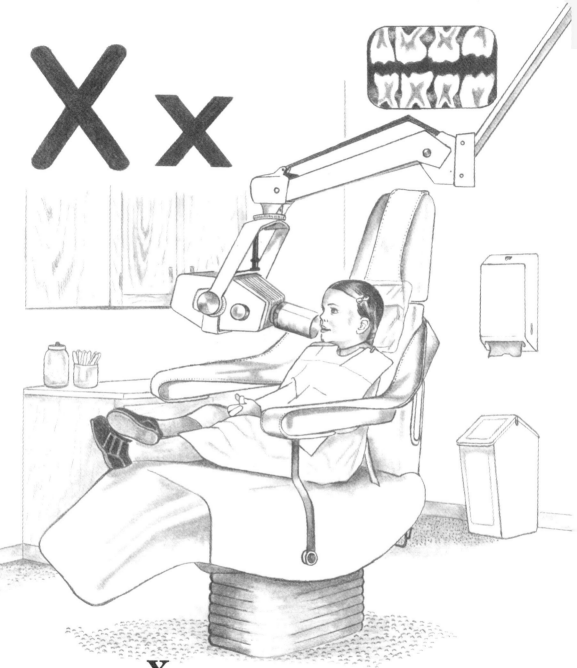

X is for the **x-rays** that
The dentist wants to take
So he can see the reason why
My tooth began to ache.

Y y

Y is for some **yellow** things
We often see in spring–
The daffodils and crocuses,
And meadowlarks that sing.

Z z

Z is for the pleasant **zoo**,
  Where people like to go
To see the birds and animals;
  God made them all you know.

A
B
C
D
E
F
G
H
I
J
K
L
M

N
O
P
Q
R
S
T
U
V
W
X
Y
Z